ANIMAL LIVES
The Rabbit

Illustrated by
Bert Kitchen

Written by
Sally Tagholm

KINGFISHER

The farmer has gone home and the rabbits have the field to themselves. The brown buck sits on guard, his long, battle-scarred ears able to pick up the tiniest sound. His big eyes scan the hedgerows; his little nose trembles and twitches in the evening air. The rabbits have not strayed far from home. They graze peacefully through the sweet grass, sprinkled with clover and starry daisies.

S uddenly the spell is broken. With a heavy thump of his strong back legs, the buck sounds the alarm. Danger looms as a buzzard circles high above, inspecting the tranquil fields for his supper. As one, the rabbits freeze, then turn and race for cover, pounding across the smooth green turf at top speed. The hungry bird of prey plummets down, claws outstretched. Too late. The speedy white bobtails reach home just in time, diving through the grassy holes that lead into their sandy warren, safe and sound.

The maze of tunnels and burrows stretches far into the side of the hill, with plenty of room for the entire colony of rabbits. There are several secret ways in and out, and some special bolt holes in case of emergency. These are just big enough for rabbits to squeeze through, but too small for most predators. After all the tender green plants that they have nibbled, the rabbits produce their first droppings – soft, round pellets of only half-digested food. There is still plenty of goodness in them, so the rabbits tuck in again and swallow them whole, enjoying a second meal. Tomorrow, when they venture out of the warren, they will leave their final droppings, dry and hard, above ground, like little heaps of smooth, black peppercorns.

When it is time to feed outside again, the buck peers cautiously from the shadowy mouth of the warren, checking the coast is clear. Only then do the young rabbits and does hop out into the fresh spring air. The buck is especially wary – and not just of predators. It is the breeding season and there may be other males on the prowl, waiting to pick a fight over one of his does. He marks out his territory to warn off his rivals, rubbing his chin against plants and twigs and sliding it along the ground, leaving a strong scent trail.

Although he has fathered several different litters already this spring, the buck is ready to mate again. He chooses a young doe, dancing round her to see if she is interested. At first, she plays for time, not quite sure. Then, with a quick flick of her little white tail, she joins in the game. They chase each other round and round, this way and that, lolloping and leaping through the long grass.

It is not long before the complicated game of catch is over. The rabbits sniff each other, their noses twitching, ready to mate. They are quite safe – no rival males around and the rest of the rabbits grazing safely in the next field. The doe gives the signal, crouching down low on her belly and lifting up her hind quarters into the air. The buck climbs on to mate. Afterwards he topples over, roly poly, onto the ground beside her. They relax quietly, side by side, a soft, browny grey bundle in the long, green grass. From time to time, the buck gently licks the doe, his long, pink tongue tenderly preening her face and ears. They drowse peacefully together, the late spring sun warming their whiskers.

The doe starts work on her nest, just outside the main warren. She digs down, her front paws flinging out a stream of sandy soil under her belly. It is hard work and, as she excavates deeper and deeper, she has to turn and heave the earth out with her chest. She makes the "breeding stop" as comfortable as possible, lining it with a mattress of old leaves and grass and patches of velvety, green moss. She even pulls tufts of short grey fur from her tummy to make a soft, warm bed.

When they are born, blind, deaf and naked, four weeks later, the helpless babies sleep quietly in their safe, dark nest, cocooned from the outside world. The doe creeps back each night to feed her litter, then slips off again into the darkness. She scratches the earth behind her, camouflaging the entrance from hungry predators such as badgers, stoats and weasels. The babies start to grow, sprouting fur as well as tiny claws and teeth in only a week. By now, they can hear each others' squeaks. Very soon their beady brown eyes will open.

By the time they are three weeks old, it is quite a squash in the nest and the growing brood are ready to investigate the world above ground. The doe stands guard as the five young rabbits peep timidly out of the burrow for the first time, then hop, one by one, into the sweet fresh air. Safe under her anxious gaze, they play with each other and explore the field, nibbling the grass.

The rabbits often come out to feed at night when fewer predators are on the prowl. Sometimes, they hop right round the farm to the vegetable garden where there are neat rows of baby lettuce, carrots and peas. But they must always have their wits about them and they stay very near the burrow when the moon is bright. They are just the right size for the old barn owl who lives in the woods and swoops silently over the fields looking for juicy morsels. The doe sticks close to her young, guarding them well and teaching them to be alert to the slightest sign of danger. Soon, she will have to leave them to fend for themselves. She has mated again, and must start work on another nest for her next litter of babies.

The five young rabbits must be careful now that they are on their own. There is an army of enemies lurking in the fields and hedgerows. The rabbits are especially wary of the big brown fox who is slinking through the farmyard and worrying the hens. He is hungry and the sight of so many plump young rabbits tempts him out into the fields. Stealthily, he creeps near, pressing low on the ground, but the rabbits are too quick. With a thump on the ground, they hoist their white tails in the air, signalling danger to each other, then bolt for cover.

All five rabbits are strong and healthy and, despite all the dangers, they should survive. Before the end of the summer, the young does might even have babies of their own and the warren will spread its labyrinth of tunnels and burrows deeper into the side of the hill. Soon the young bucks will be ready to set off and explore. One day, they will probably start colonies of their own.

THE RABBIT

Scientific name: *Oryctolagus cuniculus.*

Nicknames: Bunny, coney.

Size: Adult head to tail length up to 400mm.

Weight: Up to 2kg.

Distribution: Europe, Australia, New Zealand, United States, South America, Africa, Asia.

Habitat: Grassland, woodlands, cultivated fields, sand dunes, salt marshes, mountains, moorlands, cliffs.

Food: Grass, clover, sorrel, daisies, roots, agricultural crops, young trees, garden vegetables. Can eat 0.45kg of fresh green food daily.

Breeding: One buck (male rabbit) mates with several does (female rabbits). Litters of 2 to 8 kittens (rabbit babies) are produced at monthly intervals, mainly between January and June.

Predators: Eagles, hawks, owls, ravens, crows, buzzards, black-backed gulls, foxes, badgers, stoats, weasels, ferrets, dogs, cats, humans.

Relatives: Snowshoe rabbit (an American hare), pygmy rabbit, bristly rabbit, Mexican volcano rabbit, brown hare, antelope hare, Cape hare, cottontail (in North and South America), Blue Alpine or mountain hare, woolly hare, red rock hare, Riu-Kiu hare.

HISTORY OF THE WILD RABBIT

Rabbits were originally found only in northwest Africa, Spain and Portugal. They were a valuable source of meat and fur, and were introduced to most of the rest of Europe about 800 years ago. Much later, they were taken to other parts of the world such as Australia, New Zealand, and North and South America. They were probably introduced to Britain by the Norman invaders in 1066. Before long, most country estates in Britain had a rabbit warren, looked after by a warrener who used ferrets to chase the rabbits out of their burrows. Over the years, some rabbits escaped into the wild, and with their astonishing rate of breeding, soon became a pest to farmers.

RABBIT POPULATIONS

Rabbits are able to produce litters once a month, so rabbit populations can get very large indeed. Farmers use all kinds of methods to control the numbers, including ferreting and shooting. In the early 1950s, a deadly viral disease called myxomatosis arrived in Europe, Australia and New Zealand. First found in South America, it was introduced as a way of controlling the rabbits that were wreaking havoc on crops. The rabbit population was nearly wiped out. A tiny number survived and became resistant to the disease. These numbers are now increasing.

RABBIT WORDS

bolt hole refuge from danger

breeding stop short nesting burrow outside the main warren

buck male rabbit

burrow hole or tunnel dug by rabbits for shelter; to make a hole or tunnel

camouflaged merged into the background and hidden from predators

colony extended family of rabbits that live in a warren

doe female rabbit

droppings round pellets of digested food

graze to eat grass

kitten a baby rabbit

litter a group of baby rabbits

predator animal or bird that kills and eats other creatures

preening smoothing the fur

prey animal that is hunted for food

warren network of tunnels and burrows where a colony of rabbits lives

USEFUL CONTACTS

World Wide Fund for Nature
Panda House, Weyside Park,
Godalming, Surrey GU7 1XR
Tel: 01483 426444

Council for the Protection of Rural England
Warwick House, 25 Buckingham Palace Road,
London SW1W 0PP
Tel: 020 7976 6433

The Wildlife Trusts
The Kiln, Waterside, Mather Road,
Newark NG24 1WT
Tel: 01636 670000

Council for the Protection of Rural Wales
Ty Gwyn, 31 High Street,
Welshpool, Powys SY21 7YD
Tel: 01938 552525

Scottish Wildlife Trust
Cramond House, Kirk Cramond,
Cramond Glebe Road, Edinburgh EH4 6NS
Tel: 0131 312 7765

INDEX

ACKNOWLEDGEMENTS

The author and publishers thank Muriel Kitchen and John Tagholm for the photographs on the jacket.